God Left The Window Open

Open

A book of moments that almost meant something

Utkarsh Thaokar

BookLeaf Publishing

India | USA | UK

Dedication

To everyone I met—
You built this book with your kindness, chaos, and
collisions.

Preface

This book is what happens when you eavesdrop on your own thoughts for too long and start thinking the universe might be doing the same. God Left the Window Open is a compilation of poems, apologies, questions, and small rebellions because maybe the draft from that open window was trying to tell us something.

Acknowledgements

This book exists because of the countless words I've absorbed from the pages I've turned, the blogs I've devoured, and the voices of this generation's poets that have quietly, and sometimes loudly, shaped my thoughts. Each idea, each fragment of inspiration, has left its mark, influencing every line and every verse. This work is the sum of all the things that have sparked something within me.

Chapter 1. Ants and Other Priests

I am the least alive thing in the garden
The grass is tumbling outward like the spilled skin
of a goddess whose name we have forgotten
Ants roaming leading removers of dead creatures
while the rest of life survives by their mercy alone
And all that holy rest within the bamboo,
branches straight and curled with a perfect spherical
bubble
giving itself to millions of ants, insects, and birds
Here I watch myself evaporate into the tiniest fragments
There is less of me now than there was a second ago
disappear bit by bit, and it is almost magic
and almost dismemberment in slow motion.
I scratch my name on the bamboo
and wait for it to whisper tender thoughts.
Look at us, brilliant blooming things,
I am the same as you now.

A Brief Account of My Descent (with Footnotes)

I am falling.
At first, it's a suspicion
the breeze whistles a little too hard in my ears,
the horizon tilts like a drunken painting.
Then confirmation:
my stomach has relocated to my throat,
and time, that stubborn mule, has decided to sit down
and sulk.
Everything slows.
Now we can begin.
Air resistance: noticeable.
Roughly 9.8 meters per second squared—
the earth is calling, politely at first.
Bones brace.
Organs shift like furniture in a house that's just learned
it's haunted.
And right now, g feels like a god with no sense of humor.
I catalogue the sensations.
Skin peeling back like pages.

Cheeks rippling like loose flags.
Lungs—undecided. Breathing is less a reflex and more an
act of civil war.
Heart—missing. Possibly escaped early.
Pressure builds behind the eyes.
Behind the ribs.
Behind the memories.
And for a moment, a quiet one,
Ego: disassembling at terminal velocity.
Dignity: presumed dead on impact."
I think:
"So this is it."
"This is how the story closes."
"Not with a bang, but a freefall."
I try to pray.
Instead, I remember a math teacher telling me
"You won't always have a calculator in your pocket."
God, how wrong she was.
But even that won't help now.
The ground approaches
like a disappointed parent.
I sigh.
And then—
snap.
Elastic rebellion.
A gasp from the gods.
I'm yanked back into the sky like a secret.

It wasn't death.
It was bungee jumping.
(I was supposed to know what I was getting into)
The laughter rises faster than I did.
My scream comes second.
Then again.
Then again.
I realise:
Falling isn't the scary part.
It's the brief suspension in between,
the part where you think you've understood the world.
But the world has surprises.
Somewhere between the drop and the rebound,
I learn something
unpredictable,
unprovable,
but utterly true:
I've never felt more alive

My Tongue Was Born Pregnant

My tongue was born pregnant.
Heavy with generations of unfinished thoughts,
ancestral footnotes dangling off each vowel.
No sooner did I learn to speak
than I began to explain myself
to furniture, to flies, to God,
to people who never asked,
to people who should have.
Every sentence I begin carries twins:
one, the story I mean to tell
and the other, a screaming echo
of someone I've heard before.
It is not speech.
It is survival.
It is my mother, her mother,
and all the women before her
who weren't listened to
stuffed into my throat
like a nervous bird

building a home where silence should be.
When I talk,
my jaw forgets it has hinges.
It unspools like a film reel on fire.
Thoughts rush out like fugitives
fleeing a prison I didn't build.
My mouth doesn't move
it hemorrhages.
And oh, how I try to hold it back
tie a ribbon around a hurricane,
ask the sea to keep a secret.
But the words come anyway,
ripe and relentless.
Somewhere between my molars,
every apology I never needed to say
makes a nest.
I once tried silence.
It tasted like wet metal
and Sunday guilt.
It stuck to my teeth
like my father's quiet
which is to say,
not silence,
just a protest without witnesses.
When I fall asleep,
my dreams narrate themselves.
There is no peace.

Only paragraphs.
So yes—
My tongue was born pregnant.
And the child it carries
isn't meaning,
isn't the truth,
isn't even language.
It's the ache of needing to be understood
before I'm even finished
becoming a person

The Last Thing the Wind Remembered

I met a man whose coat was stitched from yesterdays.
He warmed himself on memories of verses
no one would buy.
He told me he used to believe in applause,
in great halls, gold-leafed names.
Then he believed in bread.
Then he believed in nothing.
He laughed when he said it,
a laugh so sharp it could have cut silk.
"The kings built their monuments,"
he said,
"and they rot."
"I built my poems — and they rot."
"But mine rot sweeter."
He lived off odd jobs and kindness.
He slept under the statue of a forgotten general.
He whispered rhymes to the cracks in the pavement,
so that even the stones would know
someone once cared enough to sing to them.

And when the last cold came,
and the city pulled its coat tighter,
the wind picked up his final lines
and carried them beyond the streets,
beyond the courts,
beyond the kings
right into the mouth of time.

Likewise

I told a friend I feel like a ghost with receipts,
living proof of purchases I never wanted.
She said, Likewise.
I said I lie awake at night and trace the spine of meaning
with a cracked thumbnail,
waiting for God to yawn or speak or just roll over.
He said, Likewise.
I confessed that love feels like a borrowed coat
warm, yes, but stitched for someone taller, thinner,
and built to leave.
They said, Likewise.
Everyone says likewise.
When I say I am collapsing in quiet places
behind bus stops, inside elevator silences,
under the weight of my own name
people nod, likewise,
as if we are sharing recipes for ruin.
I wonder,
was there a first man who said "Likewise"?
Who heard a scream and echoed it politely?

Who turned empathy into a hand-me-down,
a shrug-shaped gospel?
I ask:
If we all suffer the same affliction,
has anyone ever survived it enough to offer a cure?
Or are we just recycling the same grief,
changing the fonts, dusting it off for dinner parties?
If your pain is like mine,
and mine is like his,
and his is like hers
where is the one who isn't saying likewise,
but therefore?
Where are the people who followed the question
all the way to the back of the cave
and returned not with a mirror
but with fire?
Tell me
is likewise a comfort,
or just a room we all sit in while the house burns?

Inheritance

Maa loves to talk—
as if the tongue were a riverbed,
and every drop of silence a drought she's sworn to end.
She relates things—
faster than light bends, faster than thoughts clot—
and with an eerie precision,
as if she'd already lived our stories in some parallel
kitchen
with the kettle forever on.
Father says it's divine.
That words fall from her like manna.
But even God must rest on the seventh day.
Maa never did.
Not when grief came in, not when love packed a bag.
She kept speaking.
She spoke through heartbreak like it was a sore throat.
Michael Scott would die a thousand awkward deaths.
But she'd resurrect them all—
with a story about a neighbour's dog that once choked
on socks

just to make a point.
Yesterday, my sister said a sentence,
and I hijacked the vehicle halfway,
took the wheel,
and drove it off the plot.
I couldn't stop.
The thoughts burst out
an umbrella turned inside out by the monsoon of
memory.
My tongue a tyrant.
My mind a rogue pianist
smashing keys just to hear the echo.
Words over words,
like stitches trying to hold together a skin
that insists on splitting.
She touched my hand,
my sister,
the ghost of patience,
and said:
"That's not what I meant."
And silence fell
the kind that rings in your ears like shame.
And suddenly, I knew.
This is what Maa must feel
bones itching under skin,
yearning to push out
just to be heard.

Not for attention,
but survival.
Words not as decoration,
but as exorcism.
I am her child.
A second-hand echo of a first-born storm.
A confession made flesh.
And maybe,
just maybe—
Father is right.
Maybe it is a god's gift.
To speak so much
and still feel
there's something
left
to say.

Chapter 2. Manifesto, In Case of Emergency

They scream their gods from rooftops
But whisper when asked what those gods mean.
They tattoo ideologies on tongues,
spit slogans like scripture,
But cannot quote compassion,
Cannot define dignity without naming a tribe.
They hoard knowledge like money—
not to share,
But to sell.
The shrinks and saints now sit in the same studio,
offering trauma-healing bundles at 20% off.
Buy now. Bleed later.
Even pain has a promo code.
And the truth?
Truth's a trend, darling.
It updates weekly.
I walk through this city of neon temples,
LED altars where we sacrifice
attention spans and original thought.

A generation of noise
worshipping the loudest megaphone,
and calling that "truth."
But—
click.
The tone shifts. A bell.
We've reached cruising altitude.

An In-Flight Announcement
Good afternoon, dear passengers,
And welcome aboard **Flight 404: Meaning Not Found.**
In case of existential despair,
oxygen masks of poetry will descend—
Breathe deeply before helping others.
To your left, you'll see the emergency exit,
past the Instagram therapist
offering enlightenment in three swipes.
Pull the lever gently. Or scream. Both work.
scream identity like battle cries:
I am this, I am that,
He is my God, She is your blasphemy
Meanwhile, no-one won't instruct you,
Why their holy books whisper
Of mercy more than murder
Your seat cushion can be used
to drown quietly in introspection.
Please avoid using it as a platform

to argue on the internet.
Today's in-flight meal
includes paradoxes, false gods,
and microwaveable morals.
The seatbelt sign is on.
Buckle your doubt tightly.
This ride is not smooth.
Faith may be lost.
Time may collapse.
But your apathy is not refundable.
Should the cabin lose pressure,
You may experience clarity,
followed by a brief
and beautiful rage.
If you are still awake upon landing—
which is unlikely—
Please collect your belongings:
a half-forgotten self,
a handful of questions,
and the courage to disturb
Whatever universe they built
without you.
Thank you for choosing
to think while flying.
We know you had no choice—
But you still listened.
And that, perhaps,

is enough
to survive the fall.

A Man half-made

"Do I dare disturb..." I forget the rest
I have only dared to keep breathing.
The city was wet with neon and need,
People hurrying toward warm machines,
Eyes blue-lit, faces pixelated prayers,
Swiping for God with trembling thumbs.
I walk between coffee shops and cracked gutters,
My shoes remember the mud more than I do.
And I—An unmade man, Half-formed in ambition,
Half-sure in purpose, looking for something soft in a
world that sells steel.
And there she stood like a quiet answer
to a question the world refused to ask.
She loved the same poetry I used to fear,
Wrote in margins, stared long at birds and buildings,
Knew how to disappear without apology.
I loved her in the way a storm loves a hill.
That is to say, I meant to touch her,
But mostly, I reshaped myself instead.
I believed in God once.

Still do, on quiet mornings when my phone is dead
And no one is watching.
I light incense for no reason,
Forgive people who never knew I cursed them.
I even say 'thank you' To the silence after the music
ends.
But the world runs on invoices, not incense.
And no one forgives your rent.
They tell you to manifest.
Hustle. Grind.
Be a man.
Buy a plan.
Build your brand.
I... I wanted to breathe beside someone
And call that a life.
She left, and I did not follow
Not in defiance, but the quiet grief of two languages
Learning that they cannot be translated.
Like cities forget rivers
Gratefully, then permanently

Now, The café chair wobbles beneath me.
A stranger laughs behind a screen.
The temple down the street is now a gym.
Everyone here is sculpting
What they cannot understand.
And I sit with a silence

Too wide to hold in my chest,
Wishing meaning came
With clearer instructions again

The Noise That Follows

...Now, I speak to pigeons
And paint my thoughts on napkins
I've started drinking water like it's wine.
Started praying with my eyes open.
Started writing poems, but I never finished.
Meanwhile, men argue over flags like children over
broken toys.
They dig graves with hashtags,
Send drones like postcards of grief.
Their God wears a different uniform every century,
And still bleeds when no one is looking.
They speak of honor—But what is honor
When the widows share recipes for survival,
And children learn how to hide before they can spell?
They shoot for power, but die for nothing.
A statistic printed in bold,
Then forgotten like passwords.
The war is everywhere.
In boardrooms and bedrooms.
In temples and timelines.

In what we take, and what we never give back.
They say we are winning.
But I've seen victory
It looks a lot like loneliness wearing a suit.
Still, I walk.
Still, I breathe.
Still,
I wonder if silence is just God clearing his throat
Before he tells me what to do.

The Blood of the Earth

They came with hands that had never known what it's
like
to squeeze the breath from a man who fought in the
dust,
to hold his body as it twitched in the dark.
They came with clean collars and political speeches,
replacing the blood on the land with the perfume of their
own making,
and we were told to smile,
told to wait,
told to **thank them** for giving us the freedom
we never asked for,
that they never **earned.**
You see,
they never asked the earth what it wanted.
Never saw the way the soil cracks under its own weight,
the way the roots push **sharply upward** like a fist in
defiance.
They don't understand,
violence is **in us.**

It's written into the air,

etched into the rocks,

and coursing through our veins.

The trick is not to shut your eyes and beg for peace

the trick is to **see it, embrace it,**

and channel it.

Because when it comes,

and it will,

there's no stopping it.

You either burn or you burn.

And they ask for **nonviolence,**

as if we are meant to bow to a world that doesn't know

how to stop killing.

Do you think **that** was freedom?

Do you think sitting at tables, while men die for your

word,

and drinking tea in silk-lined rooms,

was the cost of sacrifice?

Do you think that was the **true struggle**?

While they bled for their own ideas,

they doused us with **words.**

Cheap, empty promises.

Like salt on an open wound.

Do they think they can give us the world on a silver tray,

when it was **already ours**

but they stole it?

They say, **violence breeds violence,**

but nature doesn't care for such lies.
Violence isn't bred,
it's in our bones.
Like fire in the forest,
it moves where it will,
whether we like it or not.
The land we walk on **knew it first**
knew that it would burn,
and knows the taste of blood better than any saint.
And we,
we who learned too late,
we fought and bled
to a world that told us it **could've been different**.
But nature is **violent**,
and so were we.
And we will **remain violent**.
Until the **right violence** is remembered.
Until the earth reclaims what it's owed.
And maybe, just maybe,
we will be ready to build something real

Chapter 3. The First Crack

In the corner house, behind peeling shutters,
laughter bloomed like stubborn weeds in a garden.
We spoke in riddles, all twisted-up smiles
and stories that grew tall, like the vines
we once tangled with our bare hands.
Elders with quick, clever hands
who taught us to turn a coin,
to dance in the rain
as if the storm were ours to command.
The afternoons were not quite ours,
but there, in that room too small for all the joy,
we took what we could from them
a little joke, a little warmth,
a glimpse of the happiness
that slipped into the cracks between their words.
They spoke of places I would never see,
of lives too full to contain.
Their laughter came with edges,
but I could not see them then,
not with my small eyes

not yet touched by the weight of their silence.
But the corners of that house
that house where I first felt the world
press its warm hands into my chest,
are now hollowed by ghosts
a place once alive now withered in the light
of something that was never spoken.
And as I walk these rooms full of memory,
the ghosts circle me like whispers
left in the spaces between breaths,
their laughter drowned
in the cracks of old walls.
A house, once full,
now left to echo,
echo the weight of words unsaid,
of joy,
of everything taken.
First birthday,
first tears
they are stitched into the fabric of the walls,
they don't exist anymore.

The First Eclipse

I was built by the ones who rode storms
Men who swung their victories like lanterns,
and laughed loud enough to break ceilings.
Men who planted mango trees with their bare hands,
and taught the rivers to bend for them,
or so it seemed.
He won.
He won again.
He carried fame in his pockets
like loose change.
The daughters called him king.
His sisters used to say "You are the mischief stitched into
our childhood."
The house grew fat on his triumphs.
But somewhere between the laughter and the ledgers,
between the broken-in leather and the last applause,
something cracked
so silent even his shadow didn't hear it.
And when the news came,
it didn't walk.

It ripped through the summer afternoon,
clawing at the kitchen walls,
making my mother crumple like paper.
They said no one saw it coming.
Not even the ones who kissed him goodnight.
The man who knew how to charm the rains,
the man who made summer feel like a song,
was gone.
And all the mango trees stood stunned,
waiting for a hand that would never return.
No farewell,
no final message,
just the thud of a heart folding in on itself.
My mother still carries him like a fever.
Talks to walls he might have leaned on.
Forgets her own name sometimes,
but never his.
And I —
I carry her.
I carry the ghost inside her ghost.
I walk with the dust of all their unfinished wars on my
shoulders.
Sometimes,
when the lights hum too loud,
or the road smells of rain and burning rubber,
I wonder —

am I just another house waiting for the crack to split me
clean in two?

31

The Man Who Made My Summers

There was a man once,
and in his pockets, the first rains, a broken mango seed,
a toy soldier marching into June afternoons,
the smell of books breathing through the torn screen
windows.
He was summer,
spilling kites and glass marbles across my childhood.
He built a house with his bare hands
stone, laughter, games, the first bite of ice cream melting
too fast
he built it all,
out of zero, out of less than zero,
while the world watched with its arms crossed.
But time,
time which no hand can throw stones at,
came and whispered: *Give me your dreams, your name,*
your empire.
He gambled for a second summer, and lost.
The monsoons came too late that year.

Money fled him.
Eyes once filled with pride turned glassy, suspicious.
Love soured into blame.
The empire cracked,
and the man who built summers was left standing
among the ruins
like a scarecrow the crows no longer feared.
He asked for help.
And the world, all dignified, looked away.
It is easy to be loved when you are winning.
One night,
he left,
taking thc whole season with him
the mangoes, the first rain, the small victories, the
unfinished games.
All of it, folded into a note we will never be brave
enough to read.
The earth does not scream when it is ripped open;
it only spills its red sorrow quietly.
He was not a failure.
He was a seed that bloomed when no one believed.
And when the drought came,
he did what nature sometimes does
collapsed into itself, too proud to beg for rain.
It is easy to preach peace.
But the bones of this world
know violence like they know breath

not a choice,
but a heartbeat.
I still walk past those summers sometimes.
I see his hand, scattering marbles into the dirt.
And I wonder,
if the same rivers run under my skin
what drought waits for me?

The Woman Left Behind

In the mirror, a woman fastens her smile
with rusted pins, each morning.
Behind her, the house sighs, a tired heart
walls lined with photographs of other faces,
prettier smiles, husbands with softer hands.
She once bloomed like monsoon flowers,
quick and startling, yellow against the mud,
out-talking the stars, out-dancing her own fate
but the judges in their armchairs awarded her sister
the blue ribbon for simply arriving.
There were stitched dreams tucked in her suitcase,
maps inked in secret — Paris and Bombay
but she chose a man with kind, work-worn hands,
who built small, honest walls against the wind.
And she smiled, and she smiled.
(The wallpaper learned to listen for the cracks.)
Later, the message came — a name erased by a noose of
water,
and the rooms shifted, doors swelling shut,
her mind a bouquet of black flowers opening slow.

What would have happened, she asks the ceiling,
if the blood had run differently,
if the bottle had broken elsewhere?
Now, the ghost of the other life
taps on her window at night.
Sometimes she opens it.
Sometimes she talks back.
In this unfinished house,
she roams, a woman left behind by ships,
by sisters, by weather, by gods
sewing her voice into curtains, into clocks,
into the bones of a son
who watches too closely,
and wonders, without asking,
how long before her silence
learns to call his name

Ashes In The Blood

The fields cough up rusted tools,
names buried under broken harvests
grandfather, mother, uncle, ghost
stitched into the thorns of old hedges.
We inherit hunger, fevers, unfinished songs.
They called it pride,
when the sons dragged their shadows across the mud;
they called it duty,
when the daughters stitched shut their bright mouths.
No one mentioned the slow killing of wonder.
Patriarchs drowned in their whisky at night,
and mothers, drunk on velvet myths,
broke their teeth gnawing through prayers.
We children built kingdoms from brittle bones,
crowning ourselves with splintered dreams.
The poets lied.
The heroes lied.
The gods, too, wore grief like secret armor,
and we bowed and kissed their cracked feet.
Tell a boy he must never bleed;

tell a girl she must always heal.
Crack open the orchard
watch the black roots strangle the sapling.
What legacy is this?
A war of tongues and absences,
a marriage to loneliness,
an inheritance of broken hymns,
carried like wedding gifts too heavy to lift.
Maybe the myth was never the serpent,
nor the apple,
nor the fall
But the stubborn belief that suffering makes you pure.
If there is a fixing, it is quiet:
in small betrayals of the old ways,
in laughing where silence was demanded,
in reaching for each other with scarred, stubborn hands.
Still —
when I kneel among the fields,
pressing my ear to the dirt,
I hear them whisper:
"It is your turn now.
What will you make of this graveyard?"
And I cannot answer,
not yet.

Since 2006

When you were little,
and the world was cracked open
by the sound of our parents fighting
I'd whisper, "Let's play hide and seek."
And you'd hide your face in my lap,
while I counted loud enough
to drown out the thunder in the other room.
Mama was a ghost walking through daylight,
eyes full of stormclouds she couldn't name.
Papa was a silence with sharp corners.
I was eight. You were two.
And somehow, I was the one who made you laugh.
I remember you laughing.
Even when the floor shook with rage,
you giggled from behind the curtain
like the monsters were part of the game.
Then I left.
Packed off to boarding school
while you were still learning how to spell "sister."
It was just a few cities away,

but it may as well have been Saturn.
You started growing up
watching me from photographs,
phone calls where I spoke too fast,
or didn't call at all.
You started following my music tastes,
my mannerisms,
tried to draw dragons the way I did.
You were learning love
through mimicry.
And I—I was busy trying to survive growing up.
Busy collecting friends I don't remember now,
chasing girls, losing sleep,
and forgetting you were watching.
Forgetting I had someone who believed
I was worth becoming.
Eight years of difference.
Eight years of silence in little pieces.
Eight years of coming home and noticing
how tall you'd gotten,
how quiet.
And still, I mocked.
Teased you for being "too emotional,"
too this, too that.
Like love was something to toughen out of you.
I didn't see
how the age gap had become a canyon,

and my ignorance, the wind that deepened it.
I didn't see
how your love was shrinking quietly
under the weight of all my absences.
Later that night,
you showed me your dinosaur drawing,
and I said, "Nice,"
like that was enough.
Like your art could survive my apathy.
I didn't understand then
that everything children give
is a love letter we haven't learned to read yet.
When our parents scolded me,
you stood beside me
shoulders square,
jaw clenched like mine.
But when they left,
I told you it was your fault.
You believed me.
That was your second mistake.
Because love makes children stupid.
It makes them sponges for things
they never caused.
Years passed,
and you watched me break things that weren't yours.
Phones.
Rules.

People.
Myself.
And you stayed.
I grew fluent in silence,
spoke in shrugs and half-smiles
you learned the language just to stop expecting more.
I wonder if that's why you don't ask for my help
anymore.
If my silence
is what taught you how to build walls
from old promises I forgot to keep.
Now you're taller than me. Almost taller
You don't need a cape,
or bedtime stories,
or my hand in the dark.
But I still see you
in the back of every dream
I can't hold onto
small and drowning and salt-stained
and always slipping away
before I can say the thing I should've said.
You:
with your candlelight heart
and armor made of apology receipts
you never made me cash.
You:
with your forgiveness

folded into paper planes
that still fly back to me.
You:
who probably saved me more times
than I'll ever admit.
And me?
I was never the superhero.
Just a kid with a bedsheet,
tired arms,
and a mouth too full of guilt to say "I love you."
But if you're still listening,
still waiting,
still willing
maybe tonight
we could untangle the cape,
share the blanket,
sit by the window
and let the night come with all its monsters.
Maybe this time
you can be the one
who says,
"Nothing's going to hurt you.
I promise."
Because I believe you now.
I believe you

Chapter 4. Like Thunder, Like She

I like the way you walk into rooms
like they owe you answers.
like God left a voicemail,
and you're just here to return the call.

I like the way your eyes dart—
not nervously,
but like they're scanning the room for weak logic.
like someone might say something patriarchal
and you're ready with the scalpel.

I like how you speak
sharp, funny, fatal.
like every sentence is a protest sign.
like you're always mid-rally,
and I'm the accidental crowd
clapping too slowly,
too late.

I tried once
to match your stride,
to say something about revolution
that didn't sound borrowed.
but you caught the library stamp on my tongue.
said: "don't quote Audre Lorde
if you've never felt rage in a supermarket."
and I laughed,
because of course you're right.

you're always right.
like a storm that gets the math right.
like thunder that shows its work.

I like the way you look at me
like I'm an unsolved crime
curious, enthusiast,
and already halfway to mansplain.

but then you stay
sometimes.
for a minute.
for a cigarette.
for a theory about love
that you'll un-write tomorrow.

you let me orbit.

not close enough to land,
but enough to see your heat signature
on the side of buildings,
enough to believe
the moon follows you home
out of respect.

I don't believe in soulmates.
but I believe in you
the way churches believe in wine,
even if it stains.

I think you might be the prophecy.
not the fairytale kind,
but the type written on the backs of receipts
by poets who never paid their bills.
i think you might be
what Plato meant when he got drunk
and started whispering about forms.

I like the way you argue.
like love is a footnote.
like kindness is suspicious.
like if you ever said "i miss you,"
you'd need to write a peer-reviewed paper to back it up.

and still—

here I am.
rewriting my hands
just to touch your name correctly.

The Alter Boy And The Alchemist

I brought her tulips—red, riotous things,
their heads flaring like open wounds in a chapel.
She called them charming,
and placed them beside the mirror
where I could watch them wilt in silence.
She has a cathedral for a mind.
Stone-cold, echoing with clever riddles.
I enter barefoot, naive as incense,
a boy who thinks faith is enough.
She hums to herself in Latin logic,
spins her spells in syllables I will never master.
I am all soft edges. A gullible creature
built from kindergarten glue and moonlight.
She is geometry—sharp, exact,
a theorem dressed in lipstick.
Her laughter is a scalpel.
She cuts me,
then hands me the gauze.
I thank her.

She knows how I bow.
How I fetch and fetch
like a dog with a PhD in longing.
She calls it sweet.
She calls me sweet.
Like arsenic is sweet,
if the jar is beautiful enough.
And yet,
when she says my name
even once
it trembles through me
like psalms through a broken choirboy.
Sometimes I think
she keeps me not for love
but for the pleasure of being adored.
Like a painting hung too high
to touch, but low enough
to watch you ache.
And I?
I study her.
Like a book I was never taught to read,
but quoted anyway.
God, what a genius she is.
To make me feel chosen
as she rears her glass smile,
as she dangles her voice like a rosary
I dare not kiss.

Still,
if she asked,
I'd swallow the sun whole
and apologize for the indigestion.
Perhaps this is the choice I make,
consciously like a fool signing his own
love letters with ink that burns.

Chapter 5. Wheels

First, a tricycle, proud and red,
feet pushing like a drumbeat.
I flew in circles on the driveway,
a king of three small wheels.
Then a bicycle, bigger, meaner
it threw me down, and I threw it back.
But I stayed, I stayed, I stayed
until the road and I shook hands.
Then a mopet that hummed like a happy bee,
then a bike that roared like a small god,
then a car, heavy as a sleeping animal,
that obeyed only when begged just right.
I thought:
hard work can beat anything.
Grip tighter, go faster, stay longer
and every road, every machine
would open its mouth for me.
But time
Oh, time.
Time does not open its mouth.

Time does not care for begging.
You can race it, fight it, cry at its heels
it only watches, quiet, amused.
Still —
I push the pedals,
I turn the key,
I drive the road that's left to me
because what else is there?
And when time wins,
(when it always wins)
at least it won't say I stopped riding

A Mirror The Size Of Earth

Someone once said:
we are just echoes
bouncing off the walls of time.
But I think we're more embarrassing than that
like a song no one asked for,
playing on repeat
in a room full of people too polite to turn it off.
We arrive in bodies
half-written by others,
their regrets still folded in our DNA
like bad instructions in a flat-pack cupboard.
They taught us how to bow, how to wince,
how to say sorry when we're right.
How to be brave but not too brave.
How to dream in quotas and marry in silence.
This isn't nihilism.
It's worse: it's knowing
there might be no reason,
but showing up anyway.
Maybe that's the miracle.

That the houseplant still turns toward light,
that lovers still wait at platforms,
that a stranger picks up another's dropped scarf
as if it were holy.
Not gods,
but people patching old beliefs like garments,
carrying rituals in grocery bags,
adding new customs like software updates
each bug fixed with a lullaby,
each glitch forgiven at a wedding.
We are the version 10.4.3 of some ancient pain
that still dreams in Sanskrit and speaks in memes.
Only our faces,
trying to look like they belong here.

The Music, Folks

And yet—
somewhere between the mourning and morning,
between a scream and a lullaby,
we hear something
not a truth, not a commandment
just a rhythm.
The pulse of the thing itself.
It asks for nothing,
but it is always playing.
I caught it once,
between the yawn of a bus conductor
and the last sliver of light on a rickety swing.
A sound without a throat.
The kind of music that holds your name
without ever needing to say it.
No scale could measure it,
no metronome could discipline its chaos.
It was everything
wind chimes in a storm,
the ticking of your mother's watch

as she forgets your name.
Climbing it felt like Everest folded in a song
the air thinning into prayer,
every breath a drumbeat,
every blink a cymbal crash.
And then I knew:
you do not beat the absurd.
You dance in it.
You do not fight the silence.
You hum along.
You live like it's a raga
composed by time and mistake.
And the only way to make it through
is to become the music.
It's all music, folks.
Even the static.
Especially the static.

www.ingramcontent.com/pod-product-compliance
Lightning Source LLC
La Vergne TN
LVHW021238200726
843509LV00012B/1520